Whispers in the Wind

poems by

Amelie

Green and White Publishing
Sturgis, MI

In memory of
my father,
Albert R. DeFluent

Table of Contents

From

the

Heart

INLAND

I'm homesick for the beaches
and the reaches of the sky,
for nearness of great creatures
in depths beyond the eye.
I think I hear advancing wave
and see the swirl of foam,
and something in the surge of it
recalls cell's early home.
I long to board a sailing ship
and watch the planets rise,
with nothing but the wave's lift
to wall me from the skies.
Soon I must leave the pavements,
the city's motored roar,
to stand, however briefly,
on some lonely stretch of shore,
regaining sensed connection
with Life's generative core.

REQUEST

Give me the winter strong. I will not take
More shelter than I need, lest coddled soul
Lose its communion with the planet's swing.
Let me be kin to all the staying birds,
The folded buds, the burrowed harboring—
Enough, but no more shield against the snows
Than gives my heart resurgence for the spring.

ENDEAVOR

Here is the idol broken.
Here is where the music stopped.
Here is where the colors spilled.
        —Let the fragments lie.
        —Let the tangle stay.
        —Let the dullness set.

            Then look up!
The path to the mountain
            runs far out beyond—
The chart to its treasure
            remains within the heart.

MOODS

I'm not content with anything tonight.
A wind is at the window of my heart,
And questions, sharply like a needling rain,
Strike at the pane.

And will I find their answer in the light?
I smile, because I have no need to ask.
One looks across a shadow in the sun,
Forgets with a task.

WISTFUL

Listening Heart,
You ever know all the little thoughts that go
Flashing swift or still and slow
Across my soul.

Knowing Eyes,
You ever see all that's deep and really me
And for flaws that should not be
Exact no toll.

Tender Lips,
You ever tell a love to all distresses quell,
That all life's beauty can compel
And make me whole.

PLEA

This is my garden plot;
Why won't you wander in?
Lacking your word of praise,
The beds grow thin.

DELUSION

Perhaps that was no star which seemed to ride
Along this mountain's empty ragged rim
As I looked up to view it from below.
Some lesser gentler slope whose mild ascent
Invites the quickening passion of the sun
And brings to birth from out its warm brown sides
The green of grass and unpretentious flowers,
Wind-tossed and common to all careless eyes,
Had proved a wiser choice. What blooms I saw
Had flowered in my heart, sunned by my hope,
Ere ever I commenced this vacant climb,
Which brought them death, and me to look upon
But barren ridges of blue-crevassed snows!

RAGE

I stride on fury's mountain
Protected by no cloud.
The streamered lightning flashes,
My anger is my shroud.
All dreams have been defeated,
The early bud decried;
Hurled to dust my banners,
Tramped the youthful pride.
More than form is freedom,
And faith a noble prize;
The truth within a spirit
Is sight beyond the eyes.

DOUBTED

I'll not take your fear, I cried bravely;
    I'll know it no more
Than the heart of a gull that is flying
    alone from the shore.

Alas, for pinions assailed
    before they can rise;
Young wings hesitate, waver—
    the high blue dream dies.

TURBULENCE

The night is wild and windy
    full of a kind of terror,
    and I am alone,
    longing for you,
My heart's heart, whom I cannot claim;
    to whom I may not cry nor call,
    nor turn—nor speak
    one least small word—
While longing becomes eternity,
    whirled on the tables of time
    past all joining, all acknowledgment
    and realization—
To scatter forever,
    lost as the passing wind
    strewing its fury in the night.

MEETING

I feel like the desert after rain—
To wait so long is nearly to forget
    the bloom that comes.
Thirst is a habit, slake but a moment,
    —a memory—
Engulfed with burning.

REMINDER

Let me but remember
        that I lack the time to weep:
    There's a sunrise,
        or a full moon,
            or a bird going over—
A violin is singing,
        or the bees hum
            in the clover—
Each instant
        ripening harvest
            for the living heart to reap—
The eye must see ...
    The ear must hear ...
        The moment will not keep.

SUNSET IN THE CITY

I know that it was lovely
    for I saw
High in the dusking sky
    a rosy cloud.
That alone was all;
City buildings hid from me
The brilliant blaze of the West.

CONNECTIONS

Sense now the feel
    of ever-rolling sphere,
The burst of birds in flocks
    at autumn dawn—
Consider First Man watching—
    and making a dance of it.

CAUTION

Best not go into attic rooms
Where past is stored and webbed with Time.
There will be griefs like soft grey shawls,
Folded down in loose-latched chests,
Which shaken out will take the shape of moments
Charged with tears. Old words that hurt like burrs
Caught in the wool, more cut than scratch
To recollect. And pain from loss of kin,
Or pets, where comfort, trust , and love
Were like safe respite against fate's
Unabated slap. There are the questions
Of one's own self there: Did I fail the
Small, bright, lively dog we left
For the futile call of war? I see him still
Swimming when he jumped our boat, drowning
In the river's strength, but saved when we
Turned back and took up the gape ourselves.
Later, how could we have left him?--especially
In question, he so ill and needing us
To stay. And that other, also quite misjudged
Through our preoccupations when we might
Have saved her, had we but heeded the plea
Plain in her eyes. It's like my mind to turn
To animals. I've come to know them as not less
But more than we ourselves, who share essential
Pattern, but no safeguards.

>>>

Caution, cont.

Besides all these, there are the half-done
Things, from dreams to knitting, and forgotten
Songs that never matched a meaning. Leave the
Attic. Tulips are in bud. Earth by
Grand design, has reached the Spring, and
Old longings only score the bone.

SONG OF AWARENESS

I do all that I can
        to continue reminded
Of Time and the Universe,
        and long rivers flowing—
Of seas, rock, and sand,
        the shifting of Ages,
While patterns of Life
        were changing and growing—
Cell, form, shape, and structure;
        frond, fin, paw, and hand,
Through myriad variables
        yet to be spanned ...

DOCUMENT

The plum and purple gull-wing sea
Purls and surges ceaselessly,
Plotting patterns still to be,
While at his files of A-B-C
Man records the extent that he
Pares at the rind of destiny.

Age and era, rock and shell
Note the shape of the mutant cell.
Pen-line, surf-line, dip and swell,
Scribe and carve the line to tell
Fared it long, triumphant, fell,
Slow and carefully, marking well.

Shift of rock and lift of wave
Decide the evidence to save.
Set your number by your name,
That sands may count and score your game.

QUIPU

The Years fly,
hitching by on knot by knot
of Days.
The halted Present
seems infinity of matter
and concern
that sings or slays.
But go the years
till Gone is Now,
and Past
stands up
brief as a slammed door.

POSTSCRIPT TO AN ADDICT

Oh!—I meant to tell you!—
When I came this morning to your door,
Just outside within a spot of sun,
There lay a snake, a small one—
The sort you'd make a pet of—
Quite round-eyed and harmless.
He was aware of me before I saw him,
And lay straight out and still,
But kept me in his eye.
I turned my step to leave him undisturbed
And came on in to tell you.

But I found you gone upon this trip so far
Your chair had all but overturned upon you,
And your gaze was distant—and ancient as Cathay.
I did not show the little serpent to you,
Lest you view it through some scarlet dream,
As dragon, or advent designed to harm you,
In the symbol humankind has cast it.

When I looked again, I thought it vanished.
But then I saw the snake had moved somewhat
And fetched its head full half-length off the ground,
As if to sight the way that Man had gone.

BEREFT

To destroy what we do not know—
    this is our deed;
The edge of a thing must show—
    this is our need.

The tiger stalks the padded jungle dark
    by instinct sign.
The patterned song bursts from the winging lark—
    endowed design.
Man only, asks—and being patternless,
    climbs high and falls,
Reaching for certain answers in a guess
    of human walls.

CRYPTO—

Only where the riven rock is,
    Only where is broken stone,
Group to celebrate the presence
    Of the fragile human bone.
Make device for cry and crisis,
    Roar in steel or silken tone,
Store infinity in chaos.
    Shrill together. Scream alone!

SUNRISE!
(or What Toy is This?)

Our beautiful burning golden sun!—
Amid all the mysteries of Space,
What is the Spirit, what is the Power
Expressed in a momentary grace
Of multibillion-patterned balance
On a tiny sphere in a perfect place?
Incredible miracle? God-mind plan?
Meant for challenge to mind of Man?
Our importance: are we to believe it?
Or live in awe we are here to view it?

When sun's bright glory fades and dies,
Will our planet wander the full dark skies
Seeking another fiery tether
With other Life and other Weather?

EARTH CENSUS

Walk in the ruin early
While hope still holds a question on the sign
And hate is a crack in the glaze,
Seen only in improper light—
    (which improperly prevails.)

Walk past the gaze of dreamers without plans.
This is the time of autumn leaves for plans,
    and bitter fires.

What's to come is no man's plan,
But an old certainty that comes to seedless fruit
While we engage in doomed philosophies
As futile as the rites that are put down
By that old rite of birth—
    which multiplies all desperation.

REVERENCE

O, Earth and Air, that I am part of you,
    part of your dust and dew,
    this is enough.
    More grace I could not bear.
I will not ask, *Is* God? nor *What?* nor *Where?*
That I have form and plan on such a planet,
    with eye and ear and touch
    —and sense to see—
    I am content to be.
Let not one instant's loss be chalked against
    some lesser concept than Infinity.

1991—The Gist of the Time

We have to be together now.
No nation can be alone.
The world is one for all of us,
Not separate parts to own.
Allegiance to the whole of it,
No separate part for claim—
This consciousness in each of us
Should now be constant aim.
One government for all of us
Make now our first objective,
With boundaries blent, resources shared
In one complete connective.
Respect, regard for differences;
The names of creeds discount.
Any claim of greed or grasp,
Each nation must dismount.
This finite Earth cannot divide,
But to all as equal give,
If Man, or any creature here,
Or Earth itself, shall live.

THE ROAD TOWARD HOME

Do not turn and follow—
I would travel this road alone,
With dense woods and birdsong,
And moving very slowly.
All the boughs surround me
With the breath of where I belong,
For here I touch in spirit
With every paw and stone,
And here, if any place is,
Is where the Earth is holy.

PETITION

I pray you—when this life is through,
    do not enclose me among the dead,
                the gone.
    Let me live on in wing, leaf and song.
    You who hold my ashes in your hand,
    I beg you to understand.
  Bear me back to my home hill
    and spill me there where root will find
    substance still within my dust.
  Then with the thrust of Spring
    these cells will rise in leaf and blade,
    know sun and shade, insect pattern
    and bird wing,
    may bloom and sing.
  Include me in this cycle still,
    on my home hill.

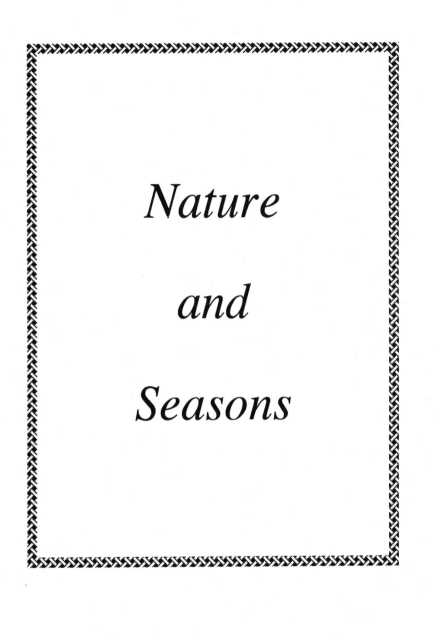

Nature

and

Seasons

BIG BANG? —
THE SHRUG OF GOD?

When Spring first trails
    her fragile veils
        of misty green
            across the World,
Bearing in the seeds of Time
    design of leaf
        and twig and vine
            up from the mold,
Cell by cell, the patterns climb
    to an order new and old
        from origins untold,
            manifest and manifold.
Question, seeker, sentient now
    in the order where you dwell,
        whence the form of bird and bough
            if not Eternal Presence tell?

SPRING SONG OF THE CARDINAL

From your bright throbbing throat
Each jubilant whetted note
Sounds new and clear;
Still on the lingering snow
Your wings make flaming show
But the springing year
Quickens from winter rest
Song in your scarlet breast,
And the barren tree
Stirs in its clinging dream
Hearing of Spring's full theme
This first sweet key.

SPRING

The tulips have been glorious this year!
I saw them on their first day
    when their colors were new and young
       and their hearts still dark
          and petal-cloistered.
Then they sprang tall,
    bearing their beauty proudly,
       each bright cup brimmed with sun.
Last night in the early twilight
    I walked beside them to say good-bye
       and thank you for this year.
The old petals are curled, still clinging,
    reluctant to give way to the iris
       on the other side of the path.

PURPLE MARTINS/COLD SPRING

We wait for wings that scamper up the air
      in little tricks of flight
           like acrobatic hallelujahs—
                the eye's delight to share.
We listen for talkative song dappling the morning sun
      from six to sixty throats,
           all trills and runs
              and unexpected notes—
The spill of a glinting joy
      in cascades of elegant fun.
           Until the martin house is filled
           the summer's not begun.

SPRING SQUALL

Confused lost flakes
    of late spring snow
Move back and forth
    upon the air,
Like lagging sheep
    trying to discover
Which way the flock has gone.

FORSYTHIA

Spring laughed
outside my window
and the sound
became entangled
in the branches
of some bushes
and there it changed
to thousands
of little golden bells.

FIREFLIES

Over the quiet garden
dreams of the rooted flowers
quicken the dusky shadows
in salute to the distant stars.

I commit my soul unto these—
     Lilac-laden boughs and new leaves.
     These my heart believes.
From whatever hidden thing
     Their life and color spring,
     My soul finds wing.

SUMMER NIGHT

Beneath full moon
the round lake lies—
a rippled platter
of hammered silver,
with wild ducks
and reeds slim
deftly wrought
along its rim.

DECEMBER TULIP BED

When this curved bed
     is bright again with bloom,
I will remember
     how it lay tonight—
White with frost
     more whitened by the moon,
Its secret color
     cloistered from my sight.

SUMMER CHANGE

Summer loves the world
With singing birds and silver moons,
A brook's wild babble,
And a wind's soft tunes

Comes pagan autumn trailing
A pair of yellow wings.
A careless song, and wanton,
With ruby lips she sings.
At summer's bier she pauses
And heaps it high with flowers,
Then turns to woo a waiting world
With gay deceitful hours.

LILACS

How beautiful, how beautiful, how beautiful are lilacs!
They cast upon the gentle wind their lovely purple sigh.
    Here they remain alone upon the land
    Where long ago some tumbled house has stood,
    And all the human hearts that sheltered there
    Are in the memory of this blossoming wood.
How softly, oh, how softly lifts remembrance on the wind
That stir among the lilacs when the springtime passes by.

SUMMER SONG

I saw a butterfly die—
Folding its sun-warm wings
    To the irreversible shadow.
Close to a nodding flower,
    Still in the sun, it fell softly,
    Just at the edge of the meadow.
Like an imperceptible sigh,
    Floating resignedly downward,
    Stilling its colors gently—
I saw a butterfly die.

OVERHEARD

Contrary jay, blue as a harebell—
   despite the winter wind,
      just for a moment sings
      a thread of song,
        secret and wild—
A strain to catch the ear
   with an eager "What-is-that?"
      and bring me to the window
      in surprise.

He quickly flees my sighting with a scream,
Jeering the very day, like some rough boy
Suddenly aware he'd mused becharmed
On poetry he had not known he knew,
And now denies the mock of alien theme,
Lest he reveal too much and lose his guise.

ENTERPRISE

Christ, I bring you the blood of swallows,
And weak small wings that missed their chance to fly.
The broken bluff, mawed by the cold machine
That crushed the safe dark pockets of the nests,
Is strewn to make a beach with boats to rent
And cottage lots to sell.

You know, of course, the place was all swamp once,
A place of many wings and many songs,
And over it the swallow-broidered bluff.
Now with the Earth's trust broken, all are gone,
For Man has come and coin is needed
To make the woods fit place to carol You.

So you take the swallows, Christ,
With their untried wings and their unsung songs—
You are familiar with the sorrows of the slain.

YOUNG TREE

The branches of this tree lift like a prayer,
This small tree, this walnut, scarcely reaching
Twenty feet above its hillside roots.
At its fork, two boughs curve out distinctly
Then midway turn to meet at tips again,
Not centered but tilted gently southward
In a gesture like petitioning hands
Toward the season shifting of the sun.
This all is clear in winter bareness now—
A prayer in the curved pattern of a leaf,
Holding the cells that promise greening spring
In trust for summer's gift of song and wing.

HOUSEWORK

Quiet for a moment!
There is some urgency to dust, is there?
To scrub and wash the windows?
Clean the closet?
Just beyond the door the asters bloom,
A flaunt of summer under autumn sun,
True urgency against the press of time.
Step out there now and look!
Brief beauty makes good claim against the broom.

DUSK TO DAWN

Out in the cherry trees
Swung from the pointed leaves
The spiders spin.
Netting their chosen spans,
Bridging the air with strands
Of silk drawn thin.

From the horizon line
Fog will creep and climb,
And bind the night,
And by the dawn will trace
Each radial-patterned space
In beaded light.

THE BABY

Infinitesimal spidery grace,
Frail as a wisp of dream,
She has wrought in this tiny
                    chosen space,
To geometric scheme.

RESIDENT

In my kitchen window's
crisply-curtained square,
a small invading spider spins
her iridescent snare.

CAT
(Kitsir)

You sit assembled neatly,
>your tail around you curled,

Compacted quite completely,
>like a little single world.

MOUSE

>I have a little mouse—
>>I hear him speed

>His little skittering steps
>>against his need

>To find some creviced sanctum
>>from my eyes.

>I have a friendly heart—
>>He does not know

>That he could stay to watch
>>and need not go,

>While I fix him dinner
>>just his size.

SPINNER

In perfect patterned space
>the spider works,

and paradoxically
>in beauty lurks.

The fog will come to jewel
>the web it spun

with beads of dewy light
>to snare the sun.

AUGUST MORNING

How silently the fog has crept
In upon us as we slept.
It dims the church's tallest spire
And blinds the firefly's white fire.
It glistens greyly on the leaves;
Its gathered mist drips from the eaves.
The whole wrapped land awaits the drift
Of morning winds to make a rift
To clear away the milky night
Before the sun's clear golden light.

OCTOBER

The moon began it full and loitered high
Into belated quiet dawn to find
Deep in the placidity of waters
Confused bewitchment with reflected round.
Between the mirror and the sphere there flew,
Like a measure or a severance,
In solemn horizontal, great blue herons,
Back and forth above the dying lilies,
Shadows of their wings reminding water
The peaked and tireless pattern of a wave.

And when the moon was old the stars shone out
As newly bright as though they'd just been set,
While midway up the month Orion blazed
Above the East earlier than midnight.

And color! For all the month the earth
Had special union with the sun, a love
Gone past the need for passionate begetting,
Mellowed, complete in its own qualities,

>>>

And every autumn hue a part of it.
First the hickories, that this year held their gold
Incredibly long, against the vibrant sky.
At the tips of branches, maples turned
Carnelian, standing candle-set for days
Before the full change dyed their waiting boughs.
The leaves of oaks turned gently rose and wine,
And finally sear, to whisper, like squirrel ghosts,
In the wind.

Late days broke forth with storm that challenged trees
And thrust the silver lances of its rain
Hard at the wind-pressed flanks of dry-grassed hills.
Through a hood of cloud-cap black as anger,
Split the concentrated wrath of lightning.

Or rainless winds cut currents in the lake
That turned it the blue-black of deeper waters.
The piling waves burst open at their crests
In frothing foam that slid away in bubbles
To sleek oblivion in the troughs between.
Gulls, stayed for moments by the rushing air,
Were motionless as brush-strokes on the scene,
White balanced curves against the thinning trees,
Unyielding till their dauntless wings attained
The distances their daring eyes achieved.

>>>

As well make count of falling leaves to tell
All the tossed moments of this enchanted time—
Not to forget that gauzy cloud that trailed
Back from the high point of the sharp young moon,
Like a veil that floats from a hasting bride;
Nor far-bound geese a-cry in dusky heavens.
Speak, too, the night aurora swept the skies,
Like vapors rising from a brew of rainbows;
And, the cast wreath of summer's vanished hand,
Those bright last marigolds and royal asters.

And now once more the earth swings down
Against a rounding moon, three-quarters showing.
The month's full wealth is almost wholly spent.
Last night was filled with chill illusive light
That minted single moments into frost,
To leave as final coinage
This brittle silver morning.

OCTOBER PRAYER

O, make my heart a cache to hold
    This day's clear wealth of gold—
A color store that will deny
    The frost-constricted days that lie
Between me now and April's arch
    Of pussy-willow sky.

MAPLES IN OCTOBER STORM

See how the golden color startles out—
    wind-whipt flame against a cobalt blue.
Were ever boughs as densely black as these
    that press gold leaves against this ardent sky?—
This sky that hugs the hills with vibrant light
    which gathers from the gold its inner fire.
The glad bright burning on this ridge of hill,
    like bright commitment of a living heart,
    rejoiced and glorified, is gathering
    of element to element, remembering
That in vast union lies a coming spring.

BEFORE HUNTING SEASON

This remains of silence—these few hours—
When golden woods make haven for the small.
Their warm brown trails across the autumn earth
Lie undisturbed by any but their feet
Which scarcely stir the leaves through which they pass.
The amber oaks show where the acorns lie,
Sweet, plump, and burnished for their garnering.
The yellow hickories shed rich bounty down
Frost-ripe and ready to make winter store.
No sound within the woodland tells the gun
That finds its mark among the higher boughs,
Nor blue October sky bears any sign
That this safe peace will break its certainty.

WINTER NEWS

The days are printed when there's snow,
When every footfall makes a show
Of ways our woodland neighbors go.

Here hopped a moon-struck cottontail,
And over there is the starry trail
Left by a covey of feeding quail.

Just beneath the hill's last rise,
A pausing deer, with wary eyes,
Assured his safety against surprise.

Leading toward a sheltering pine
Runs a dainty mousetail line,
Crossing a squirrel's well-spaced design.

Straight ran a fox by the brookside reeds,
Where a flock of juncoes scuffed for seeds
Dropped from the pods of withered weeds.

This is the language winter knows,
Written briefly upon its snows,
Going when the season goes.

WINTER BIRDS

Here they are, the mighty small,
Clinging to the winter trees,
Spreading wings to every squall,
With no plea for summer's ease.
No bird startles when jets go over
High in the blue beyond the sight;
Intently feeding where crumbs are scattered,
They spare no heed to sonic flight.
Their small wings against the blasts
Of winter winds can bare compare
In faith and strength with motored wings
Which dare the spans of higher air.

THE TREE

With all the bright affairs of Christmas past,
This is the morning when the tree comes down.
The needles make a carpet of their own,
All slippery on the carpet of the floor.
Ribbons, baubles, tinsel...all are packed.
Where once the white star graced the highest tip
The twig is dried and naked of its green.

There's little quite as dismal as a tree
Left standing all forlorn beyond its time,
Held captive past the brink of the New Year,
A tethered spirit whose bright breath was drawn
Fresh in the cheer of Christmas. Let it go.
Placed against the earth and given fire,
Its form will lift again within the flame,
A scarlet spire rising from the snow
To join the elements from which it came.

FUN
WITH
BIRDS IN RHYME

A is for avocet
   active and agile;
His slim legs are strong
   although they look fragile.
And for flipper-winged auk
   on some sea rock he sits on
With his strange razor bill
   that appears to be stitched on.

B is for bunting
   blue as a banner,
Or his cousin who's painted
   in carnival manner.
It's also for bluebird,
   blackbird and bob-o-link--
One warbles, one whistles,
   One lilts "plink-a-plink."

C is for cardinal
   crimson and crested,
And for chickadee, too,
   black-capped and white-vested.

D is for dove
    and for duck and dickcissel;
The first mourns, the next dives,
    the third sits on a thistle.

E begins eagle
    who soars in the sky;
He nests on a cliff
    where the wind whistles by.
E's also for egret,
    white fisher of shallows--
On sighting a fish,
    he spears it and swallows.

F is for finch
    who frolics in flight,
And sharp-billed, speckled flicker,
    whose tail flashes white.

G is for grosbeak
    lovely of song,
For grackle whose tail
    is keel-shaped and long,
For gull and for goose
    whose beauty in flight
Give any who see them
    a sense of delight.

H begins heron,
 who fishes with grace,
  And flitting bright hummingbird
  too swift to trace.
  Hawk is another
   who belongs to this letter;
  Don't hate or condemn him
   till you know him better.

I is for ibis,
  a marsh wader shy,
 Who lifts in magnificent
  throngs to the sky.

J is for junco
  in a monk's cowl;
 He'll come for your crumbs
  when winter winds howl.
 J is also for jay,
  big, bright, and so blue;
 It's sad that his manners
  are not lovely, too.

K is for kinglet,
    top-knotted and pert,
For the rugged, bold kingbird,
    too careless of hurt,
For rowdy, ringed killdeer
    who calls from the clearing,
And comic kingfisher,
    diving and peering.

L is for lark
    a lyrical triller,
As well as for loon,
    whose call is a chiller.

M is for martin
    the big purple swallow,
And the gay meadowlark
    whose bib is bright yellow.

N begins nuthatch,
    natty and sassy;
Winter won't daunt him,
    with spirit that brassy.
(And what do you think of his name?--
    it's a queer one;
He doesn't hatch nuts,
    though his harsh voice might shear one!)

O is for oriole,
    elegant singer;
In a high hanging nest,
    he begins as a swinger.
Owl is another
    beginning with "O";
His call from the night woods
    Is muted and low.

P is for peewee,
    plaintive and hidden,
And for pigeon most bold
    who will visit unbidden.
Q is for quail,
    quaintly checkered, and calling
"More wet," foretells rain
    which soon will be falling.

R is for robin,
    robust and red-breasted;
There's no lack of song
    where robins have nested.

S is for sparrow--
    song, tree, and white-throated
Plus some fifty others,
    (Not "house," be it noted!)
This latter's no sparrow
    though he goes by the name;
It's carelessly given
    and brings the rest shame.

T begins titmouse,
      small grey-crested mite,
Whose cheery sweet whistle
      is a winter delight.
T, too, is for thrasher,
      tailored in brown,
Who struts like a dandy
      parading the town.
Add thrush, who is shy
      except for his song,
Which spills from the hedges
      the May morning long;
Add tern, that slim waterbird
      graceful to see,
And the black, white-and-chestnut
      lovely towhee.

U,— that's for Universe
      that holds all these creatures,
All fish, birds, beasts and bees—
      plus all pupils and teachers!

V is for vireo
      rarely in view,
But his song from the treetop
      showers on you.

W rolls
     like the warbler's sweet notes
There are numerous warblers
     and no sweeter throats.
This wavy letter
     is also for wren,
And for woodpecker, too,
     who leaves holes where he's been.

X marks the spot
     where any bird's nest is;
For eggs and young fledglings,
     birds' own care the best is.

Y is for yellow-throat,
     black mask on his eyes;
His song, a quick <u>witchity</u>,
     breaks his disguise.

Z - zonotrichia,
     a long word that belongs
To a certain few sparrows
     with beautiful songs.
Among them, the ones we're
     most likely to see
Are the Harris, the white-throat,
     the white-crowned, these three.

All birds are not here
Because birds are a throng;
Counting each in the world
Does make a list long.
Each one for a letter
For a page in one book
Gets too many pages,
Has too fat a look.
It's a start to have these,
Just for finding the pleasure
Knowing can bring us,
Like song for a treasure.
Many a bright wing
Now we will see
Over the garden or
Perched in a tree;
Quick among branches,
Roving the skies,
Singing and winging
Till the day dies.
Unknown the power
Very deep in the heart
Which guides all their ways, as
X marks a chart.
Years in their seasons reliably bring
Zest of returning song and wing.

People,

Places

and

Perils

NEW SPRING

I had not thought to see it bloom again,
This bush beside the door through which she came,
White-clad and silver-haired, to gather them,
These purple flowers of which she liked to think
She was a part and they a part of her,
With life to life connected—
That they knew her touch, cherished her caress,
As she had need of their soft fragrances,
Their crisp new blooms, like pets beneath her hand.
How fortunate and sadly comforting
To know that she can never guess
The lilacs did not understand.

MOM

Silken silver head upon my shoulder—
You were not old,
    just tired for the moment;
I said the words to soothe, giving a pat—
    brace up and not to worry.
I was in a hurry. It was quick comfort,
    quickly given. I had other things
    to do than really comfort you.
Now I wish I'd loved you more
    held you longer, closer,
    made no haste—
Though in truth, haste was in part
    to make a shield
    against distress you would have felt
    for things I could not tell you.
Still, perhaps less shelter and more love—
    or more expressed,
    had I but sensed last moments
    to save last chance from loss.

MY FATHER

I long to have belonged to myself
    in the early morning.
To have known your kindred thought
    in the birth of my dawn.
What was the fate that took you
    out of my childhood
Ere ever my senses awakened
    to find you had gone?

CHILDHOOD:

    A scarlet poppy
flaming in the green
of a straight-pathed garden
open to the sun—
    a new soul
laughing under azure sky
where clouds ride
too high for vision.

Stars are children's dreams;
In their clear bright gleaming
Lie the great tomorrows
To crystal from that dreaming—
Ships that sail to lands
Of hope and come back knowing
Life anew with beauty,
    and fair winds blowing.

E.H.

Here she came seeking the gate of the garden,
Bearing her ripe and primal answer,
Warm with promise, the one fulfillment—
The waited, yearned, denied, now offered.

Under her steps, with the burning candle
Aspiring the altar, the mountain rose.
Gaining the final height, trembling and calling,
She found the gate closed.

OF VIKKI

I will tell them
    you were laughing when you passed me.
I will say
    I heard you sing a phrase of song.
Your gallantry will stay with me forever,
A wistful shield against a mighty wrong.

TO MY SOMETIME DAUGHTER

Fresh as the morning,
I hope you will be—
A rose without a thorn,
A lily, fine and proud,
   yet not disdainful
      of the crowd.
Welcome laughter—
   let it live
      within your eyes,
         its joy to give.
Love all nature—
   always be
      aware of the earth,
         the sky, the sea.
I want you to have
   thoughts that shine
With a heart-born joy,
   daughter of mine.

BITTERSWEET TREE/MEDIEVAL MOMENT
(Dedicated to Marian, who called my attention
                 to the tree -   October 19, 1991)

O, I'm sorry to have missed your dance!
I came only just in time to catch the close—
Your draperies inward curved all down around you,
Your head inclined in gentle sidewise pose.

What instruction guided early shoots
To trace this lovely ballerina grace,
Giving you aspect which questions roots,
And lends an ancient magic to your place?

—Might visit you some roving unicorn
In early morn before day's sky's begun,
To match your breezy dance with mincing prance,
In shared salute to rim of rising sun?—

A TOY "TURTLE" BANK

This little turtle tank
    is supposed to be a bank,
though as a place to hold your money
    I'll admit it's rather funny.
It's hard to figure whether
    the idea is that savings
    for most people
        grow
            rather
                slow.
Or if perhaps it's meaning
    that when put beneath the shell
    of a creature from the past,
        funds
            will
                last.
But there's one thing I do know:
    Coins are almost sure to go
quickly out of any pocket
    since it's difficult to lock it,
while one bit at a time—
    penny, quarter, nickel, dime—
in a place where you can stash it
    and can't get at it
        ('less
            you
                smash it!)
will someday make you thankful
    when you find
        YOU HAVE A BANKFUL!

This BIRTHDAY!!!

It's not like me to look back.
    I don't feel old.
I greet the morning on the rising beam
    that sets the day aglow.
Zest is the same as when day's to-do's
    were skip-the-rope 'n' marbles,
Though richer now with love and work,
    and knowing so much more.
But all the while the sneaky years
    were toting up this score!

MANHATTAN PAUSE

I lean upon the park's stone balustrade
And gaze across the kept expanse of grass
To make myself a time unwalled and free.
I toss my soul upon the breathing earth;
It rolls across the smoothness like a hoop,
Past little urgent signs commanding "Please!"
Which make small hurdles for the skipping shoes
My hopes put on to run along behind
The spinning iridescence of my dreams.

ALIVE

Spirit needs time to climb awhile,
Moments to be inebriate with joy,
To lean idle on a handy rock or tree,
Freed of obligation's come-and-go,
To realize quickened dust and destiny.

MANHATTAN NOON: BRYANT PARK

This leafy island sanctum in the stone,
Amid unyielding pavement-patterned squares,
Scantly bears
Some fundamental startings of the earth,
The reaching root, the pregnant start of bud.

Man must return to these,
And in his rigid hour-bordered noon,
Out from his stony towers his hungered heart,
In secret, rests beneath the numbered trees
Of city parks between the static reach
Of sky-accosting, sun-eclipsing walls,
That share no primal pulse nor breath of life.

HILLSIDE CATARACT

(Upper Hector Falls, New York State)

Out from the forest wilderness,
Out to the sunlight's bright caress,
Down from the rocks of hillside home,
Your crystal waters leap and foam—

O, Sparkling, vivid stream that sings
Of cool and mystic woodland things,
Of far, dim-hidden mother springs,
Where feathered carolers dip their wings,
The song you sing the ages through
Is Nature's soul in the voice of you.

? NUCLEAR DESTINY ?

There may be no tomorrow, though we do not know—
That's just as well. A wisp of smoke, perhaps,
Where this house stands. My neighbor looks
To see a bird fly past—he is a lucky one
To look. Tomorrow may have no eyes, nor wings,
Nor even consciousness. Here children savor
Fragrant chunks of cake, and fresh milk brims
Their glass—just taste is miracle enough.
I hope they are aware of it, for taste and touch,
And all of it, may go, leaving blankness, a vacuity.
Would it take an Age, or maybe millions,
Before another creature ventured reach beyond
The elemental limits of a crawl? What irony
That Man holds leash on breath of total death!
Does it make some answer? Would there be time
Under the same sun for all to grow again?—
Over the same patterns? Would the gift of Mind
To a creature Man repeat as risk in a future plan?

WAR
? ...5000 BC ...?

Our sphere yet marks with blinded eye
Its eastward curve against the sky,
Urging a bitter destiny within a starry canopy.
Now and again the mourning breeze
Sifts tattered music through the trees.
Our sun and moon appear and shine
On transient gain of battle line,
While futile blood still spills and spreads
In wasting pools around the dead.
Yet press we on, beguiled by dream
Which fogs clear truth with things that seem
Till all the gifts that mind implies
Are lost to a demon paradise.

H-BOMB — FIRST WARNING

We consider it and say, "It might destroy the world."
As though, indisputably, Earth belonged to us.
How calm; with what temerity! Could we be proud?
The World! The Sphere?...
Spraying out in all directions,
Sucked particle by particle to other stars,
Making an alien dust, the source of which
Is indefinable. The oceans vaporized,
The mighty mountains quite disintegrated,
Ancient bones dispersed, and baby hands,
My child's red hairbow, and the scrolls
That men in thought laboriously produced,
Expanding wisdom, hopefully awake, —
The neighbor's toolshed, moon-dreamed Taj Mahal,
Our kitten's paw, the teeth of beasts that prowled
The jungle dusk in innocent savagery.

We lack that innocence. We have the world.
We see beyond our hunger and our mate.
Does knowledge lead to infinite destruction then?
We have the world...although we circle it
Like vying tigers snarling round a kill.

>>>

There was the Life, and now are we the Death?
Since God we cannot, then must we be demons?
Is it a jealousy that makes us damned?
With what aplomb we fondle fearsome things,
As if there were no cost,
And no accounting.
But then, we need it don't we?
You see, we are so dangerous to each other!
And being unequipped with fang or claw,
What better use for wits than make us weapons?
I am afraid of you and you of me,
For here behind the barrier of our skulls
There lurks the enemy...
With whom there is no reason!

BANG

—?—

GOD is a gambler
      and Life is the luck
Sprung from the dark
      of the ALL that was struck

```
                    E         e
   n           H  G         r
   i   t at    U  fr   u    o
       h            a t     f      NS
          ?         c              E  I  Y
          ?  /  ?              /    D     T
          /        / ??      ?    ?
          ?               /    ?    /
```

Is Life a Dream of Wanting-to-Be,
The Thought of a Sphere to suffice
For Pattern and Plan, from Cell to Man?—
Or the Whole just a chance device?

OF 2nd ISAIAH

It startles that these words
                designed to chide
The temper of a lost antiquity
Should fit as well the features
                of our day.
Is it forever then that Man shall be
So young in Time that his own fashionings
Will rouse in him a marvel which mistakes
That mayhap he alone is his own god?

Love,

Friendship

and

Tears

FIRST LOVE

For a short while within the quiet night
The grassy hills were there for us alone,
While far above were spread the stars more bright
And burning splendid than had ever shone.
Across our brows the dusky winds were soft.
The crickets sang and all was peace serene
Even that plane which bore our world aloft
Seemed some strange star across our moon's white beam.

Then came your kiss, a star upon my cheek,
Fleet as the wing that bears a passing bird,
Sweet as the fresh bud of a folded rose.
Between us then there was no need to speak,
And in my heart the joy the treasure stirred
Blooms like a flower and like a star it glows.

REUNION

I'll stand at the gate and search the faces.
Will I know you and will you know me?
Do aught of the early promised graces
Remain to make an identity?
Should I wear a blossom? What is for hope?—
Violet? Aster? Anemone?
Is it right that the trembling moment grope,
Or best to save chance with certainty?
What will it be when eyes meet eyes,
Will the love shine out that once was prized?

CITY LOVERS

Looking back
    it seems as if we flew
along the avenue
in a kind of iridescent flight.
A sudden gift of wings
    might have given
this same sense of heaven;
quintescent joy,a high delight,
mingled both with fountain glow
    and spire height,
till all the city belonged to us
    especially.
Each sight struck blended tone
as if our spirits owned
some complement of bells.
If such enchantment shared
    roots truth in stone,
that blossoming reveals
that no brown fields
bear greater bounty than
    these pavements yield.

FRIEND

Being with you is pleasant
   as honey on a warm biscuit,
      or piquant as good wine
         mulled and laced with spice.

I can sit in the corner of your heart,
   with my chin in my hand,
      and contemplate Life
         in the radiance of your spirit.

Or I can reach for you
   under the clouds of circumstance,
      comfortably speaking everything—
         or nothing.

Fair is the weather between us,
   bright or showered—
      friendship makes its own sun
         whatever tomorrows come.

CHANCE MEETING

May your spirit often rise
    free-winging on the winds of joy,
May all the sky-wide scene
    show beauty to your eyes:

    I have marked the dates
    secretly—
    to hold them in my mind
    and in my heart. Two sailors
    on the faceless ocean—
    a moment's surcease,
    disclosure,
      resolution,
        answer,
          insight,
            recognition,
              renewal—
    a meal of one coconut
    before recommitment to the sea.

MISUNDERSTOOD

Just not to possess—
    this is your distress,
But have you ever spoken
    a love that was not believed?
To comfort you I stole
    half of my whole soul,
And yet remained untrusted
    nor reckoned t be grieved

What I tried to give—
    a memory to live
Against your heart to hold
    the coming years.
But you returned the balm
    in bitterness and qualm.
Left to me?—a measureless
    futility of tears.

DEAR FRIEND:

I cannot even give you love
Without distressing you
And raising some dark question
Constantly obsessing you.
I cannot comfort, cannot stay
Your grief's onslaught
Nor keep the day, the heart-held hours
When I've thought
I gave as much as I could give
To help you live.

ESCAPE

I leave it to God to tell you
    the truth of my love,
And give you the comfort
    I tried to give you and failed.
The healing is there if you
    will not insist on the wound.
One may bear a cross but still
    may escape being nailed.

COMPANION

The hour closes like a closing flower
Upon the instant when you leave the door
And turn to go, with my heart smiling on you.
Then I bring out the treasures that I store
To brighten hours that are spent without you—
Your laugh, your glance, the tones that bear your words,
Your eyes grown quiet with a sudden thought—
These wing my mind as beautiful as birds.

And when at last I linger close to sleep
It finds me loathe to let the visions go.
Although I know dream hours will be fleet.
My joy is like a star that shimmers deep
Within the shadowy void of night to keep
Its watch across the time when we will meet.

WAITING

The rain came softly, sounding
like footsteps that I longed for—
(Why should I dream surely
on this night you would come?)
Let me have the peace then,
the quiet peace of rain,
in place of desolation,
of broken hope and pain.
Make me content with the rain,
loneliness and rain.

LAMENT - *(and Reply)*

Still as the years come on, you disturb me—
though with nearness no longer.
Even that seems but loss of the chance
to convince you of my love,, my hope, the worth
                                    of my dreams.
I go on, neither more nor less futile, imploring.
Thoughts are bound up with my heart,
hopeless now as from the beginning,
but longing and trying and hoping,
while knowing there can be no answer—

                    no peace and no answer.

Yeah? So—
        It is necessary for the heart to recognize
        There will be persons who will never
                            understand you:
        No amount of words serve to reveal
        Truth, intent, purpose, or your particular
                                    script!
        So cease, back off, give up, retreat—
        Likely other hearts will find your message sweet!

98

ILLUSION

I speak to you always in my mind,
Always— although you are never there.
The you that I mean, I have built myself
Of a few kind words and a long despair.
But the you that is you, I scarcely know—
And startle to find beyond the frame
Of that which longing has formed from dream
And cloaked with the magic of your name.

PROMISE

I will come to find you
Across the clouded mountain
With nothing but my need
To light and guide the way,
For you are to my spirit
As sunlight is to day,
And the lack of you
Is no cup at the fountain.

DIVORCE

I do not dream that I can speak to you
across the miles. I could not speak to you
across the table. Words were useless.
What was this dichotomy?—a divergence so profound
that neither mind nor heart could find the tongue
of it. I longed—and long—to share myself
with you, to run laughing down the ways of time,
wipe dry your tears, mend every wound, and grow
with you, loving and beloved. But no.
You turned somehow to look along an angled path.
Or did we both? Did I unwitting take an angle, too?
—so each view equally was strange to each?
Yet to be close, confiding, trusting, warm,
soothed against those flaws I would redeem,
was my whole burning hope, grown to conflagration
till all our scene was desolate as ashes,
and each of us alone.

COUNTERPART

Do not change. I cherish the thought of you
        just as you are.
I shall love you still
        when my blood has gone with the rivers
        and my breath has joined the winds.
What I feel is part of Time and the Universe—
        it can suffer, yet not be destroyed.
It is no transient thing, confined and limited—
        it has flung open the windows of my heart
        to combine my being with Eternity.

I have loved you for so long
I cannot count the time—
Or time becomes my love,
A chain of seconds,
Link to following link,
Between the jewelled hours
When you come.

Or time is like
The tall stem of a flower
Budded with dream
That bursts with bloom
More rich than all my hope,
When you are here.

TEMPTED

My heart longs for tender words to trace
The precious constant image of your face
Forever at the windows of my mind.

My reason—lest I dare presume
To give my heart's wish room
To cry, "Beloved!"—pulls the blind.

RENUNCIATION

I wish with my whole heart
I might have answered,
"No, dear, it won't be long—
    I'll come tomorrow,"
and been without a thought of
What if the morning rains?
Or knowing that the cloud
    would be there always.
Grief took me down the stairs
    abruptly—
Totally aware of the tick of Time.

NEXT DAY

One whole day has passed.
      You are not here anymore to know
      what I put on to wear.
      How am I to see myself?
Never again will you say, "I like that skirt,"
Or "That top and pants go well together," or
"That's a great shade of blue for you."
      I don't know what to choose.
When I wore it, you would say, "You like pink,
      don't you?" You didn't!—
      Pale, you thought. "A little weak," you said;
      "not red, but not white either."
      "Of course not!" I protested.
But I did not wear it for you often.

"Who's there now to say, "Hello, Beautiful!"?
      —and me at this age!
I know sometimes you said the same to others
      —yet it was not the same—
      You loved me, and I knew it.
I'll miss you. Already I know I never guessed
      how much!
I have to learn to let you be dead.
I don't see how I'll ever come to know it.
      I wish you back! I want you here!

MAIL-ORDER MUSIC BOX

It arrived after you were gone,
This little joyful gift, a touch of fun.
How like you! Thinking of me always,
Sharing laughter over china cat—
Twirling a tune, this wind-up toy—
In semblance of a creature we both love.
"Memories", they say the tune is—
Not to say I need the prompting:
You are with me hourly through each day.
How like your gentle heart to know
The time to order me this one last smile.

Joy is a bird on a wind-whipt branch,
    a butterfly touch on a finger—
A moment of instant quickened chance
    not to be trusted to linger.

HOPE

My darling, of the whole of us,
Each of us is part;
Somehow I know you're with me,
Close as heart to heart.
When I, too, cross the bridge of time,
I'll have things to confess—
So much you knew, and rightly, too,
Though I denied your guess.
As one we'll fly the ways of change,
Wherever change may lead us—
As one united energy
       may Spirit ever read us.

QUESTIONS IN A MIRROR

I've come to call you counterpart.
I wonder if you know it.
I like to think you surely do,
Though there's no proof to show it?
Or is that wrong? Can Spirit be
The thing that's truly real
And form we see, that seems?—
A figure we can touch and feel,
To give awareness means?

Acknowledgements

City Lovers - Published in Christian Science Monitor
Home Forum; Used by permission

Manhattan Noon: Bryant Park - Published in
National Poetry Anthology 1952-53

October - Published in American Weave Magazine

Request - Published in Christian Science Monitor
Home Forum; Used by permission

Spring Song of the Cardinal - Published in Christian
Science Monitor, Home Forum;
Used by permission

The Tree - Published in Heartland Journal

Winter News - Published in Colorado Old Times

INDEX

Title	Page #